DOGS

VS
CATS

Why Dogs Are
Woman's and Man's
Best Friend

Dog lovers start here

IAN BLACK

BLACK & WHITE PUBLISHING

First published 2004
by Black & White Publishing Ltd
99 Giles Street, Edinburgh EH6 6BZ

ISBN 1 84502 022 7

British Library Cataloguing in Publication Data:
A catalogue record for this book is available
from the British Library.

Cover illustration by Bob Dewar

Printed and bound in Denmark by AIT Nørhaven A/S

CONTENTS

	INTRODUCTION	5
1	WHY IT'S GREAT TO BE A DOG	7
2	BEFORE I WAS A DOG MUM	9
3	DOG vs LEOPARD	11
4	WE HAVE THE TECHNOLOGY	13
5	MOSES AND JESUS	15
6	THIRTEEN THINGS DOGS DON'T UNDERSTAND	17
7	THINGS I LEARNED FROM MY DOG	19
8	DOG HAIKU	21
9	PUNNY FUNNY DOGS	24
10	BASIC RULES FOR DOGS	26
11	DOG PROPERTY LAWS	29
12	YOU MUST BE CHOKING ...	30
13	UNLUCKY FOR SOME	35
14	DOG DICTIONARY	36
15	GREAT TRUTHS ABOUT LIFE ...	39
16	QUOTABLE QUOTES	40
17	K9 SAYINGS	44
18	THE RIGHT STUFF	45
19	HOW TO PHOTOGRAPH A NEW PUPPY	46
20	GOOD DOG	48

21 A DOG QUESTIONS GOD   51
22 THE DOG RULES   53
23 RULES FOR DOG OWNERS (SUGGESTED BY THEIR DOGS) 55
24 A CHRISTMAS WATCHDOG   58
25 A DOG'S CHRISTMAS PROMISES   59
26 EQUAL OPPORTUNITY   61
27 HOW MANY DOGS DOES IT TAKE TO CHANGE
    A LIGHT BULB?   63
28 CREATION AND THE DOG   66
29 AYE, IF   67
30 WHY DOGS ARE BETTER THAN WOMEN   68
31 WHY DOGS ARE BETTER THAN MEN   73
32 WHEN GOOD DOGS GO AND CROSSBREED   75
33 NICE DOGGIE   77

DOGS vs CATS

INTRODUCTION

Dogs aren't cool. Dogs are warm. Dogs are dogged. When a dog loves you he loves you through to the marrow of your bones and for ever. If there are no dogs in heaven, then when I die I want to go where they did.

The following was directed to a jury by Missouri Senator George Graham Vest in the 19th century and every word remains true today.

"The best friend man has in the world may turn against him and become his enemy. His son, or daughter, that he has reared with loving care may prove ungrateful. Those who are nearest and dearest to us, those whom we trust with our happiness and good name may become traitors to their faith. The money a man has, he may lose. It flies away from him, perhaps when he needs it most. A man's reputation may be sacrificed in a moment of ill-considered action. The people who are prone to fall on their knees when success is with us may be the first to throw the stone of malice when failure settles its cloud upon our head.

"The one absolutely unselfish friend that man can have in this selfish world, the one that never deserts him, the one that never proves ungrateful or treacherous, is his dog. A man's dog stands by him in prosperity and poverty, in health and in sickness. He will sleep on the cold ground when the wintry winds blow and the snow drives fiercely, if only to be near his master's side. He will kiss the hand that has no food to offer, he will lick the wounds and sores that come in encounters with the roughness of the world. He guards the sleep of his pauper master as if he were a prince.

"When all other friends desert, he remains. When riches take wing, and reputation falls to pieces, he is as constant in his love as the sun in its journey through the heavens.

"If fortune drives his master forth, an outcast in the world, friendless and homeless, the faithful dog asks no higher privilege than that of accompanying him, to guard him against danger, to fight against his enemies. And when that last scene of all comes, and death takes his master in its embrace and his body is laid away in the cold ground, no matter if all other friends pursue their way, there, by the graveside will the noble dog be found, his head between his paws, his eyes sad, but open in alert watchfulness, faithful and true, even in death."

Fido the dog

1
WHY IT'S GREAT TO BE A DOG

No one expects you to take a bath every day.

When it's raining, you can lie around the house all day and never worry about being fired.

You can wear a fur coat and no one thinks you're insensitive.

If it itches, you can reach it. And no matter what itches no one is offended if you scratch it in public.

It's okay if you never amount to anything except being a dog.

If you grow hair in weird places, no one notices.

You never get into trouble for putting your head in a stranger's lap.

Nobody thinks less of you for farting in public.

Your friends never expect you to pay for lunch, drink, or anything else for that matter.

A chew toy can entertain you for hours.

There's no such thing as bad food.

No one gets angry if you fall asleep while they're talking.

You can sleep late every day.

People think you're normal if you stick your head out the window to feel the wind in your hair.

You never have to worry about good table manners.

Someone else combs your hair.

Your mate never complains because you whine.

Everything smells good to you.

You're always excited to see the same old people.

Every rubbish bin is a fast-food stop.

And if you gain weight, it's someone else's fault!

2
BEFORE I WAS A DOG MUM

Before I was a Dog Mum –
I made and ate hot meals unmolested. I had
unstained, unfurred clothes. I had quiet conversations
on the phone, even if the doorbell rang.

Before I was a Dog Mum –
I slept as late as I wanted. And never worried about
how late I got to bed or if I could get into my bed.

Before I was a Dog Mum –
I cleaned my house every day. I never tripped over
toys, chop bones or chewy toys – or invited the
neighbour's dog over to play.

Before I was a Dog Mum –
I didn't worry if my plants, cleansers, plastic bags,
toilet paper, soap or deodorant were poisonous or
dangerous.

Before I was a Dog Mum –
I had never been peed on, pooped on, drooled on, chewed or pinched by puppy teeth.

Before I was a Dog Mum –
I had complete control of my thoughts, my body and mind. I slept all night without sharing the covers or pillow.

Before I was a Dog Mum –
I never looked into big, soulful eyes and cried. I never felt my heart break into a million pieces when I couldn't stop a hurt. I never knew something so furry and four-legged could affect my heart so deeply.

Before I was a Dog Mum –
I had never held a sleeping puppy just because I couldn't bear to let go. I had never got up in the middle of the night every 10 minutes to make sure all was well. I didn't know how warm it feels inside to feed a hungry puppy. I didn't know that something so small could make me feel so important.

Before I was a Dog Mum –
I had never known the warmth, the joy, the love, the heartache, the wonderment or the satisfaction of being a Dog Mum.

3
DOG vs LEOPARD

A man decides to go on a safari in Africa. He takes his faithful pet dog along for company. One day the dog starts chasing butterflies and before long he discovers that he is lost. So, wandering about, he notices a leopard heading rapidly in his direction with the obvious intention of having lunch.

The dog thinks, "God, I'm in deep shit now."

Then he notices some bones on the ground close by, and immediately settles down to chew the bones with his back to the approaching cat.

Just as the leopard is about to leap, the dog exclaims loudly, "Goodness, that was a delicious leopard. I wonder if there are any more around here?"

Hearing this, the leopard halts his attack in mid-stride as a look of terror comes over him, and he slinks away into the trees.

"Whew," says the leopard, "that was close. That dog nearly had me."

Meanwhile, a monkey who had been watching the

whole scene from a nearby tree, thinks that he can put this knowledge to good use and trade it for protection from the leopard. So, off he goes. But the dog saw him heading after the leopard with great speed, and figured that something must be up. The monkey soon catches up with the leopard, spills the beans and strikes a deal for himself with the leopard.

The leopard is furious at being made a fool of and says, "Here monkey, hop on my back and see what's going to happen to that conniving canine."

Now, the dog sees the leopard coming with the monkey on his back, and thinks, "What am I going to do now?" But instead of running, the dog sits down with his back to his attackers pretending he hasn't seen them yet.

Just when they get close enough to hear, the dog says, "Where's that monkey? I can never trust him. I sent him off half an hour ago to bring me another leopard, and he's still not back!"

4
WE HAVE THE TECHNOLOGY

A man brought a very limp dog into the veterinary surgery. As he laid the dog on the table, the vet pulled out his stethoscope, placing the receptor on the dog's chest. After a moment or two, the vet shook his head sadly and said, "I'm sorry, but your dog has passed away."

"What?" screamed the man. "How can you tell? You haven't done any testing on him or anything. I want another opinion!" With that, the vet turned and left the room. In a few moments, he returned with a Labrador retriever. The retriever went to work, checking the poor dog out thoroughly. After a considerable amount of sniffing, the retriever sadly shook his head and said, "Bark".

The vet then took the Labrador out and returned in a few moments with a cat, who also checked out the poor dog on the table. As had his predecessors, the cat sadly shook his head and said, "Meow." He then jumped off the table and ran out of the room.

The vet handed the man a bill for £600. The dog's owner went ballistic. "£600! Just to tell me my dog is dead? This is outrageous!" The vet shook his head sadly and explained. "If you had taken my word for it, it would have been £50, but with the Lab work and the cat scan . . ."

5
MOSES AND JESUS

A burglar broke into a house one night. He shone his torch around, looking for valuables, and when he picked up a CD player to place into his bag, a strange, disembodied voice echoed from the dark saying, "Jesus is watching you."

He nearly jumped out of his skin, clicked his torch off and froze.

When he heard nothing more after a bit, he shook his head, promised himself a long holiday after his next big score, then clicked the torch back on and began searching for more valuables. Just as he pulled the stereo out so that he could disconnect the wires, clear as a bell he heard, "Jesus is watching you."

Totally rattled, he shone his torch around frantically, looking for the source of the voice.

Finally, in the corner of the room, his torch beam came to rest on a parrot.

"Did you say that?" he hissed at the parrot.

"Yes," the parrot confessed, then squawked, "I'm

just trying to warn you."

The burglar relaxed. "Warn me, eh? Who do you think you are anyway?"

"Moses," replied the parrot.

"Moses," the burglar laughed. "What kind of people would name a parrot Moses?"

The parrot answered, "The same kind of people that would pick the name Jesus for a Rottweiler."

6
THIRTEEN THINGS DOGS DON'T UNDERSTAND

It's not a laugh to practise barking at 3 a.m.

It's wrong to back granny into a corner and guard her.

He shouldn't jump on your bed when he's sopping wet.

The command "SHUT THE F*** UP!" means just that.

The cats have every right to be in the living room.

Crapping on the floor is not something deserving of a treat.

Barking at guests 10 minutes after they arrive is stupid.

No, we said SIT.

I know it's a nice leg, but don't ride it.

Getting up does NOT mean we are going for a walk.

Just because I'm eating, doesn't mean you can.

If you look at me with those big soppy eyes, I'm not going to give in and feed you. NOT NOT NOT. Oh, OK, just this once.

No, it's my food . . . Oh all right then, just a wee bit.

7
THINGS I LEARNED FROM MY DOG

Never pass up the opportunity to go on a trip.

Allow the experience of fresh air and the wind in your face to be pure ecstasy.

When loved ones come home, always run to greet them.

When it's in your best interest, practise obedience.

Let others know when they've invaded your territory.

Take naps and stretch before rising.

Run, romp, and play daily.

Eat with gusto and enthusiasm.

Be loyal.

Never pretend to be something you're not.

If what you want lies buried, dig until you find it.

When someone is having a bad day, be silent, sit close by, and nuzzle them gently.

Thrive on attention and let people touch you.

Avoid biting when a simple growl will do.

On hot days, drink lots of water and lie under a shady tree.

When you're happy, dance around and wag your entire body.

Delight in the simple joy of a long walk.

If you stare at someone long enough, eventually you'll get what you want.

Don't go out without ID.

Be aware of when to hold your tongue, and when to use it.

Always give people a friendly greeting. A cold nose in the crotch is effective.

If it's not wet and sloppy, it's not a real kiss.

8
DOG HAIKU

I love my master
Thus I perfume myself with
This long-rotted dead rat.

I lie belly-up
In the sunshine, happier than
You ever will be.

Today I sniffed
Many dog bums – I celebrate
By kissing your face.

I sound the alarm!
Paper boy – come to kill us all –
Look! Look! Look! Look! Look!

I sound the alarm!
Postman Fiend – come to kill us all
Look! Look! Look! Look! Look!

I sound the alarm!
Meter reader – come to kill us all –
Look! Look! Look! Look! Look!

I sound the alarm!
Binman man – come to kill us all –
Look! Look! Look! Look! Look!

I sound the alarm!
Neighbour's cat – come to kill all!
Look! Look! Look! Look! Look!

I lift my leg and
Pee on each bush. Hello, Spot –
Sniff this and weep.

How do I love thee?
The ways are numberless as
My hairs on the rug.

My human is home!
I am so ecstatic I have
Made a puddle.

I hate my choke chain –
Look, world, they strangle me!
Ack Ack Ack Ack Ack Ack!

Sleeping here, my chin
On your foot – no greater bliss – well,
Maybe catching cats.

Look in my eyes and
Deny it. No human could
Love you as much as I do.

Dig under fence – why?
Because it's there. Because it's
There. Because it's there.

I am your best friend.
Now, always, and especially
When you are eating.

You may call them fleas,
But they are far more – I call
Them a vocation.

My owner's mood is
Romantic – I lie near their
Feet. I let off a big wet one.

9
PUNNY FUNNY DOGS

A dog owner in Possil, a tough area of Glasgow, had a pit bull terrier that hated to walk. He kept sitting down and bracing his feet so that his owner would have to drag him by his leash. The owner finally gave up when he realised that he was creating a . . . bottomless pit.

Jimmy had a dog that talked in its sleep and one day a visitor was astonished to hear the dog bellow, "My name is Tony Blair! I am seven hundred years old! I own America! I married Lady Diana!" When the visitor asked what was going on, Jimmy replied, "Don't worry about it . . . just let sleeping dogs lie."

A man, who wanted a dog to protect his home, visited a kennel that specialised in big vicious dogs. The man explained to the kennel owner that he wanted the biggest, most vicious dog in the kennel, and the owner offered to take the man on a tour of the premises.

After they had been walking for a few minutes, they came upon a large dog, snarling loudly, and biting and clawing at the cage.

"He looks like he'd be a pretty good dog," said the buyer.

"Well, he's not bad," replied the owner, "but I have a different one in mind for you."

They continued walking around the premises, and after a while they found an even larger, angrier dog than the first. He snarled at the two men and tried to bite them through the wire on his cage.

"Ah," said the buyer. "This must be the dog you were referring to earlier."

"Well, no," said the owner. "I have something better in mind for you."

The men continued their tour. Eventually, they came upon a large dog, panting heavily and lying quietly on his side, licking his bum frantically. He seemed unaware of the men's approach.

"This is the dog I had in mind for you," said the owner.

The buyer was flabbergasted. "You're joking!" he exclaimed. "This dog is tame compared to the others. He doesn't even act like a guard dog."

"I know he appears tame now," said the owner. "But he's just eaten a lawyer, and he's trying to get the taste out of his mouth."

10
BASIC RULES FOR DOGS

NEWSPAPERS: If you have to go to the bathroom while playing in the front garden, always use the newspaper that's placed in the porch every morning for that purpose.

VISITORS: Quickly determine which guest is afraid of dogs. Charge across the room, barking loudly and leap playfully on this person. If the human falls down on the floor and starts crying, lick its face and growl gently to show your concern.

BARKING: Because you are a dog, you are expected to bark. So bark – a lot. Your owners will be very happy to hear you protecting their house. Especially late at night while they are sleeping safely in their beds. There is no more secure feeling for a human than to keep waking up in the middle of the night and hearing your protective bark, bark, bark . . .

LICKING: Always take a BIG drink from your water dish immediately before licking your human. Humans prefer clean tongues. Be ready to fetch your human a towel.

HOLES: Rather than digging a BIG hole in the middle of the lawn and upsetting your human, dig a lot of smaller holes all over the lawn so they won't notice. If you arrange a little pile of dirt on one side of each hole, maybe they'll think it's moles. There are never enough holes in the ground. Strive daily to do your part to help correct this problem.

DOORS: The area directly in front of a door is always reserved for the family dog to sleep.

THE ART OF SNIFFING: Humans like to be sniffed. Everywhere. It is your duty, as the family dog, to accommodate them.

DINING ETIQUETTE: Always sit under the table at dinner, especially when there are guests, so you can clean up any food that falls on the floor. It's also a good time to practise your sniffing.

GOING FOR WALKS: Rules of the road – when out for a walk with your master or mistress, never go to the bathroom on your own lawn.

COUCHES: It is perfectly permissible to lie on the new couch after all your humans have gone to bed.

PLAYING: If you lose your footing while chasing a ball or stick, use the flower bed to absorb your fall so you don't injure yourself.

CHASING CATS: When chasing cats, make sure you never – quite – catch them. It spoils all the fun.

CHEWING: Make a contribution to the fashion industry. Eat a shoe.

11
DOG PROPERTY LAWS

If I like it, it's mine.

If it's in my mouth, it's mine.

If I can take it from you, it's mine.

If I had it a little while ago, it's mine.

If it's mine, it must never appear to be yours in any way.

If I'm chewing something up, all the pieces are mine.

If it just looks like mine, it's mine.

If I saw it first, it's mine.

If you are playing with something and you put it down, it automatically becomes mine.

If it's broken, it's yours.

12
YOU MUST BE CHOKING . . .

A very timid little man ventured into a bar in Glasgow and, clearing his throat, asked, ". . . ah, err, which of you gentlemen owns the Doberman tied to the lamp post outside?"

A giant of a man, wearing leathers, his body hair growing out through the seams, turned slowly on his stool, looked down at the quivering little man and said, "It's my dog. Why?"

"Well," squeaked the little man, obviously very nervous, "My dog just killed it."

"What?" roared the big man in disbelief. "What kind of dog do you have?"

"It's a four-week-old puppy." answered the little man.

"Liar!" roared the giant. "How could your puppy kill my Doberman?"

"He choked on it."

A man was in a hurry to board an aeroplane and didn't have time to do the paperwork to get his little dog on board. So the man stashed the puppy down the front of his trousers and sneaked him on to the plane. About 30 minutes into the flight, a stewardess noticed that the man was squirming in his seat. "Are you OK, sir?" the stewardess asked.

"Yes, I'm fine," said the man.

Time went by and again the stewardess noticed strange movements. "Are you sure you're all right, sir?"

"Yes," the man insisted, "but I have a confession to make. I didn't have time to do the paperwork to bring my puppy on board, so I hid him down the front of my trousers."

"I see," the stewardess said. "Well, as long as he's house-trained, I suppose it will be all right."

"Oh, he's house-trained," the man replied. "The problem is, he's not weaned yet!"

An avid duck hunter was in the market for a new dog. His search ended when he found a dog that could actually walk on water to retrieve a duck. Surprised by his find, he was sure none of his friends would ever believe him.

He decided to try to break the news to a friend of his, a pessimist by nature, and invited him to hunt with him and his new dog. As they waited by the shore, a flock of ducks flew by. They fired and a duck fell. The dog responded and jumped into the water. The dog, however, did not sink but instead walked across the water to retrieve the bird, never getting more than his paws wet. The friend saw everything but did not say a single word.

On the drive home the hunter asked his friend, "Did you notice anything unusual about my new dog"?

"I did indeed," responded his friend. "He can't swim."

A young girl is wandering through a park in the pouring rain, when she comes across three dogs. Being a bit of an animal lover, she approaches them, bends down and starts to stroke one of them: "Ah, you're lovely, aren't you?" she says to the first dog. "What's your name?" To her surprise, the dog actually answers her.

"My name's Hughie, and I've had a great day going in and out of puddles."

Delighted with this discovery, she moves on to the next dog. "And what's your name, then?"

Again, unbelievably, the second dog answers her, "My name's Louis, and I've had a great day going in and out of puddles."

And so she moves on to the last dog. "Let me guess," she says. "Your name's Dewy, and you've had a great day going in and out of puddles."

"No," replies the last dog. "My name's Puddles, and I've had a terrible day."

One day an old woman was sitting in her chair outside her wee but and ben. Beside her slept her mangy old dog, Rex. Suddenly, a genie appeared, startling the old woman. "Old woman," the genie said, "I felt sorry for you sitting here looking old and tired, so I decided to grant you three wishes."

The old woman thought about it and said, "Well, I've always wanted to be a young, beautiful princess." Poof! The genie turned her into a young, beautiful princess.

The princess thought more and said, "A princess should live in a castle, so could you do something about this old croft?" Poof! The old house was transformed into a huge castle.

Again the princess thought then asked, "Shouldn't a beautiful princess have a handsome prince?" The genie looked around and spotted Rex. Poof! Rex was transformed into a handsome prince.

"Well, my work here is done," the genie said and he disappeared in a puff of smoke. The princess gazed at Rex the handsome prince and felt her heart beating rapidly, for he was the most handsome man she had ever seen. Rex, the handsome prince, strolled up to the beautiful princess and kissed her passionately. She melted in his arms and cried, "Take me Rex! Take me now!" Rex then whispered in her ear, "You're sorry that you had me neutered now, aren't you?"

13
UNLUCKY FOR SOME

Willie got off the lift on the 4th floor and nervously knocked on his blind date's door. She opened it and was as beautiful and charming as everyone had said.

"I'll be ready in a few minutes," she said. "Why don't you play with Fido while you're waiting? He does wonderful tricks. He rolls over, shakes hands, sits up and if you make a hoop with your arms, he'll jump through them."

Willie went on to the veranda and started playing with the dog, who was rolling over and sitting up and obviously wanting to play. After the dog had gone through the rest of its repertoire, he eventually made a hoop with his arms and Fido jumped through – and over the railing.

Just then, Willie's blind date walked out. "Isn't Fido the nicest, happiest dog you've ever seen?"

"To tell the truth," he replied, "he seemed a wee bit depressed to me."

14
DOG DICTIONARY

LEASH: A strap which attaches to your collar, enabling you to lead your person where you want him/her to go.

DOG BED: Any soft, clean surface, such as the white bedspread in the guest room or the newly upholstered couch in the living room.

DROOL: Is what you do when your persons have food and you don't. To do this properly you must sit as close as you can and look sad and let the drool fall to the floor, or better yet, on their laps.

SNIFF: A social custom to use when you greet other dogs. Place your nose as close as you can to the other dog's rear end and inhale deeply, repeat several times, or until your person makes you stop. This can also be done to human's crotches.

RUBBISH BIN: A container which your neighbours put out once a week to test your ingenuity. You must stand on your hind legs and try to push the lid off with your nose. If you do it right, you are rewarded with wrappers to shred, beef bones to consume and mouldy crusts of bread.

BICYCLES: Two-wheeled exercise machines, invented for dogs to control body fat. To get maximum aerobic benefit, you must hide behind a bush and dash out, bark loudly and run alongside for a few yards; the person then swerves and falls into the bushes, and you prance away.

DEAFNESS: This is a malady which affects dogs when their person wants them in and they want to stay out. Symptoms include staring blankly at the person, then running in the opposite direction, or lying down.

THUNDER: This is a signal that the world is coming to an end. Humans remain amazingly calm during thunderstorms, so it is necessary to warn them of the danger by trembling uncontrollably, panting, rolling your eyes wildly, and following at their heels.

WASTEPAPER BASKET: This is a dog toy filled with paper, envelopes, and old sweetie wrappers. When you get bored, turn over the basket and strew the papers all over the house until your person comes home.

SOFAS: Are to dogs what napkins are to people. After eating it is polite to run up and down the front of the sofa and wipe your whiskers clean.

BATH: This is a process by which the humans drench the floor, walls and themselves. You can help by shaking vigorously and frequently.

BUMP: The best way to get your human's attention when they are drinking a fresh cup of coffee or tea.

GOOSE BUMP: A tactic to use as a last resort when the Regular Bump doesn't get the attention you require . . . especially effective when combined with The Sniff. See above.

LOVE: Is a feeling of intense affection, given freely and without restriction. The best way you can show your love is to wag your tail. If you're lucky, a human will love you in return. If not, you can always sniff their crotches.

15
GREAT TRUTHS ABOUT LIFE . . .

No matter how hard you try, you can't baptise cats.

You can't trust dogs to watch your food.

Puppies still have bad breath even after eating a Tictac.

16
QUOTABLE QUOTES

Some days you're the dog; some days you're the lamp post.
Unknown

Whoever said you can't buy happiness forgot about puppies.
Gene Hill

In dog years, I'm dead.
Unknown

Dogs feel very strongly that they should always go with you in the car, in case the need should arise for them to bark violently at nothing, right in your ear.
Dave Barry

To his dog, every man is Napoleon; hence the constant popularity of dogs
Aldous Huxley

A dog teaches a boy fidelity, perseverance, and to turn around three times before lying down.

Robert Benchley

Did you ever walk into a room and forget why you walked in? I think that's how dogs spend their lives.

Sue Murphy

I loathe people who keep dogs. They are cowards who haven't got the guts to bite people themselves.

August Strindberg

No animal should ever jump up on the dining room furniture unless absolutely certain that he can hold his own in the conversation.

Fran Lebowitz

Ever consider what they must think of us? I mean, here we come back from a grocery store with the most amazing haul – chicken, pork, half a cow. They must think we're the greatest hunters on earth!

Anne Tyler

I wonder if other dogs think poodles are members of a weird religious cult.

Rita Rudner

My dog is worried about the economy because dog food is up to 99 pence a tin. That's almost £7.00 in dog money.

Joe Weinstein

If I have any beliefs about immortality, it is that certain dogs I have known will go to heaven, and very, very few persons.

James Thurber

Don't accept your dog's admiration as conclusive evidence that you are wonderful.

Ann Landers

Of all the things I miss from veterinary practice, puppy breath is one of the most fond memories!

Dr. Tom Cat

There is no psychiatrist in the world like a puppy licking your face.

Ben Williams

When a man's best friend is his dog, that dog has a problem.

Edward Abbey

No one appreciates the very special genius of your conversation as the dog does.

Christopher Morley

A dog is the only thing on earth that loves you more than he loves himself.

Josh Billings

Man is a dog's idea of what God should be.
Holbrook Jackson

The average dog is a nicer person than the average person.
Andrew A. Rooney

He is your friend, your partner, your defender, your dog. You are his life, his love, his leader. He will be yours, faithful and true, to the last beat of his heart. You owe it to him to be worthy of such devotion.

Unknown

If you pick up a starving dog and make him prosperous, he will not bite you; that is the principal difference between a dog and a man.

Mark Twain

I've seen a look in dogs' eyes, a quickly vanishing look of amazed contempt, and I am convinced that basically dogs think humans are nuts.

John Steinbeck

17
K9 SAYINGS

It may be called puppy love, but it's real to the puppy.

I had to get rid of my husband. The dog was allergic.

I hope to be the kind of person my dog thinks I am.

If you think dogs can't count, try putting three dog biscuits in your pocket then giving Fido only two of them.

Outside of a dog, a book is probably man's best friend. Inside of a dog, it's too dark to read.

Did you ever notice that when you blow in a dog's face he gets mad at you? But put him in a car and the first thing he does is stick his head out the window.

18
THE RIGHT STUFF

There was once an aspiring vet who put himself through veterinary school working at nights as a taxidermist. Upon graduation, he decided he could combine his two vocations to better serve the needs of his patients and their owners, while doubling his practice and, therefore, his income. He opened his own surgery with a notice on the door saying, "Dr. McGregor, Veterinary Medicine and Taxidermy. Either way, you get your dog back!"

19
HOW TO PHOTOGRAPH A NEW PUPPY

1. Remove film from box and load camera.
2. Remove film box from puppy's mouth and throw in bin.
3. Remove puppy from bin and brush coffee grounds from muzzle.
4. Choose a suitable background for photo.
5. Mount camera on tripod and focus.
6. Find puppy and take dirty sock from mouth.
7. Place puppy in pre-focused spot and return to camera.
8. Forget about spot and crawl after puppy on knees.
9. Focus with one hand and fend off puppy with other hand.
10. Get tissue and clean nose print from lens.
11. Take flash cube from puppy's mouth and throw in bin.
12. Put cat outside and put antiseptic on the scratch on puppy's nose.

13. Put magazines back on coffee table.
14. Try to get puppy's attention by squeaking toy over your head.
15. Replace your glasses and check camera for damage.
16. Jump up in time to grab puppy by scruff of neck and say, "No, outside! No, outside!"
17. Call spouse to clean up mess.
18. Fix a drink.
19. Sit back in armchair with drink and resolve to teach puppy "sit" and "stay" first thing in the morning.

20
GOOD DOG

A butcher is busy at work when he notices a dog in his shop. He shoos the dog away. Later, he notices the dog is back again. He walks over to the dog, and notices that the dog has a note in his mouth. The butcher takes the note which reads, "Can I have 12 sausages and a leg of lamb, please."

The butcher looks, and lo and behold, in the dog's mouth, there is a £20 note. So, the butcher takes the money, puts the sausages and lamb in a bag, and places it in the dog's mouth.

The butcher is very impressed, and since it's closing time, he decides to close up the shop and follow the dog. So, off he goes. The dog is walking down the street and comes to a crossing. The dog puts down the bag, jumps up and presses the crossing button. Then he waits patiently, bag in mouth, for the lights to change. They do, and he walks across the road, with the butcher following. The dog then comes to a bus stop, and starts looking at the timetable. The butcher is in awe at this stage. The dog checks out the times, and sits on one of the seats to wait for the bus.

Along comes a bus. The dog walks to the front of the bus, looks at the number, and goes back to his seat. Another bus comes. Again the dog goes and looks at the number, notices it's the right bus, and climbs on. The butcher, by now open-mouthed, follows him on to the bus.

The bus travels through town and out to the suburbs. Eventually the dog gets up, moves to the front of the bus, stands on his hind legs and pushes the button to stop the bus. The dog gets off, groceries still in his mouth, with the butcher still following. They walk down the road, and the dog approaches a house. He walks up the path, and drops the groceries on the step. Then he walks back down the path, takes a big run, and throws himself *whap!* against the door. He goes back down the path, takes another run, and throws himself *whap!* against the door again. There's no answer at the door, so the dog goes back down the path, jumps up on a narrow wall, and walks along the perimeter of the garden. He gets to a window, and bangs his head against it several times. He walks back, jumps off the wall, and waits at the door. The butcher watches as a big guy opens the door, and starts laying into the dog, really shouting at him.

The butcher runs up and stops the man. "What are you doing? This dog is a genius. He could be on TV, for God's sake!"

"He's not as clever as he thinks he is," the man responds. "This is the second time this week he's forgotten his key."

21
A DOG QUESTIONS GOD

Dear God

How is it that people love to smell flowers, but seldom, if ever, smell one another? Where are their priorities?

Dear God

When we get to Heaven, can we sit on your couch? Or is it the same old story?

Dear God

If a dog barks his head off in the forest and no human hears him, is he still a bad dog?

Dear God

Is it true that in Heaven, dining room tables have on-ramps?

Dear God

If we come back as humans, is that good, or bad?

Dear God

More meatballs, less spaghetti, please.

Dear God

When we get to the Pearly Gates, do we have to

shake hands to get in?

Dear God

We dogs can understand human verbal instructions, hand signals, whistles, horns, clickers, beepers, scent IDs, electromagnetic energy fields, and Frisbee flight paths. What do humans understand?

Dear God

Are there dogs on other planets or are we alone? I have been howling at the moon and stars for a long time, but all I ever hear back is the collie across the street!

Dear God

Are there postmen in Heaven? If there are, will I have to apologise?

Dear God

Is it true that dogs are not allowed in restaurants because we can't make up our minds what NOT to order? Or is it the carpets thing, again?

Dear God

May I have my testicles back?

22
THE DOG RULES

Dogs are never permitted in the house.

The dog stays outside in the specially built wooden compartment called a kennel.

OK, the dog can enter the house, but only for short visits or if his own house is under renovation.

OK, the dog can stay in the house on a permanent basis provided his kennel could be sold in a car boot sale to a novice dog owner.

Inside the house, the dog is not allowed to run free and is confined to a comfortable, but secure cage.

OK, the cage becomes part of a "two for one" deal in the car boot sale and the dog can go wherever he wants.

The dog is never allowed on the furniture.

OK, the dog can get up on the old furniture, but not the new furniture.

OK, the dog can get up on the new furniture until it looks like the old furniture and then we'll sell the whole lot and buy new furniture on which the dog will most definitely not be allowed.

The dog never sleeps on the bed. Period.

OK, the dog can sleep at the foot of the bed only.

OK, the dog can sleep alongside you, but he is not allowed under the covers.

OK, the dog can sleep under the covers, but not with his head on your pillow.

OK, the dog can sleep alongside you, under the covers with his head on your pillow, but if he snores, he's got to leave the room.

OK, the dog can sleep and snore and fart and have nightmares in your bed, but he's not to come in and sleep on the couch in the TV room, where you are now sleeping. That's just not fair.

Remember, in any and all household interactions or disputes:

The dog rules!

23
RULES FOR DOG OWNERS
(SUGGESTED BY THEIR DOGS)

I will not bathe my dog after he bathes himself in the mud puddle.

I will not push my dog away when she wants a hug after playing in a mud puddle.

I will not complain "My arm is tired" after only throwing the ball 20 times.

I will not confuse my dog by throwing snowballs for him to fetch.

I will not ask my dog to play fetch with a boomerang.

I will not drag my dog away from the interesting sniffing spots.

I will drop whatever I'm doing and take my dog out as soon as he asks me to.

I will not tell my dog to hurry up when he's looking for just the right spot to take care of business.

I will not stare while my dog is doing his business.

I will not feed the cat before I feed my dog.

I will get rid of that cat.

I will not bring home any more cats.

I will never eat until my dog has tasted what I have and has approved it for me.

I will share everything I eat with my dog.

I will set up the paddling pool every day it's hot – even in December.

I will not leave my dog at home any time I go in the car.

I will allow my dog on the couch.

I will protect my dog from that obnoxious little human thing at all times.

I will not have another of those obnoxious little human things.

I will not hide my dog's ball in a place where I know he couldn't possibly retrieve it from and then ask him to go and get it.

I will not take shredded, soggy, yummy tennis balls away from my dog.

I will not sneak around the garden wearing funny clothes to test whether my dog is a good watchdog.

I will stop referring to my dog's necklace as her 'collar'.

I will not cut my dog's nails.

I will not abandon my dog for trivial reasons like 'going to work'.

I will not wake my dog when I come home from work.

I will not come home from work and feel the sofa to see if it is still warm from where my dog was sleeping illegally.

Bad weather is no excuse for not walking my dog.

I will open the back door as soon as my dog sits by it.

I will not laugh at my dog for being confused over not being able to find the lump of ice that he buried earlier.

I will not run out of treats.

I will always carry sweeties and treats.

I will not make my dog wear silly-looking antlers or red hats.

I will not make my dog pose for pictures with some fat stranger in a red suit.

I will not tie ribbons and bows all over my dog.

I will not use decorations like tinsel that could be dangerous to my dog.

I will try much harder to understand my dog's language.

24

A CHRISTMAS WATCHDOG

Tonight's my first night as a watchdog,
    And here it is Christmas Eve.
The children are sleeping all cosy upstairs,
    While I'm guarding the stockings and tree.

What's that now – soft footsteps on the roof?
    Could it be a cat or a mouse?
Who's this down the chimney?
    A thief with a beard – and a big sack
    for robbing the house?

I'm barking, I'm growling, I'm biting his bum,
    He howls and jumps back in his sleigh.
I scare his strange horses, they leap in the air,
    I've frightened the whole bunch away.

Now the house is all peaceful and quiet again,
    The stockings are safe as can be.
Won't the kiddies be glad when they wake up tomorrow,
    And see how I've guarded the tree.

25
A DOG'S CHRISTMAS PROMISES

Christmas is for humans, and I will not ruin the surprises by opening all their presents.

Christmas light bulbs, Christmas ornaments, Christmas stockings, and tinsel from the Christmas tree are not food.

I am the alpha dog, therefore I do not need to protect my new Christmas chew from the omega dog by taking it outside to eat when the wind chill factor is -10°F.

I will not demolish the Christmas tree and drag the string of lights out into the garden through the doggy door.

I will not dive into the Christmas tree to get the sweeties (which I will eat – paper and all).

I will not eat my Christmas doggie treats until after they're out of the stocking.

I will not even THINK about going underneath the Christmas tree and piddling on the dining room rug.

I will not get into a fight with the bigger dog next door, making my human have to call the vet's at Christmas.

I will not get tangled up in the Christmas tree lights and pull the tree down while trying to get at a cat through the conservatory window.

I will not pee on Granny's Christmas presents that are under her tree as soon as we enter her house.

I will not pee on the Christmas tree.

I will not steal the neighbour's Christmas light bulbs.

The bowl underneath the Christmas tree is not a dog dish. I will not drink from it. It will make me sick.

26
EQUAL OPPORTUNITY

A local company was looking for an office assistant. They put a sign in the window, stating the following: "PERSON WANTED. Must be able to type, must be good with a computer and must be bilingual. We are an Equal Opportunity Employer."

A short time afterwards, a dog trotted up to the window, saw the sign and went inside. He looked at the receptionist and wagged his tail, then walked over to the sign, looked at it and whined.

Getting the idea, the receptionist got the office manager. The office manager looked at the dog and was surprised, to say the least. However, the dog looked determined, so he led him into the office. Inside, the dog jumped up on the chair and stared at the manager. The manager said "I can't hire you. The sign says you have to be able to type."

The dog jumped down, went to the typewriter and proceeded to type out a perfect letter. He took out the page and trotted over to the manager and gave it to him, then jumped back on the chair. The manager was stunned, but then told the dog "the sign says you have to be good with a computer."

The dog jumped down again and went to the computer. The dog proceeded to enter and execute a perfect programme that worked flawlessly the first time. By this time the manager was totally dumb-founded.

He looked at the dog and said, "I realise that you are a very intelligent dog and have some interesting abilities. However, I still can't give you the job." The dog jumped down and went to a copy of the sign and put his paw on the sentences that told about being an Equal Opportunity Employer. The manager said, "Yes, but the sign also says that you have to be bilingual."

The dog looked at the manager calmly and said, "Meow".

27
HOW MANY DOGS DOES IT TAKE TO CHANGE A LIGHT BULB?

Golden Retriever
The sun is shining, the day is young, we've got our whole lives ahead of us, and you're inside worrying about a light bulb?

Border Collie
Just one. And I'll replace any wiring that's not up to specification.

Dachshund
I can't reach the stupid lamp!

Toy Poodle
I'll just blow in the Border collie's ear and he'll do it. By the time he finishes rewiring the house, my nails will be dry.

Rottweiler
Go ahead! Make me!

Shi-tzu
Puh-leeze, dah-ling. Let the servants. . . .

Labrador
Oh, me, me!!! Pleeeeeeaze let me change the light bulb! Can I? Can I? Eh? Eh? Can I?

Malamute
Let the Border collie do it. You can feed me while he's busy.

Cocker Spaniel
Why change it? I can still pee on the carpet in the dark.

Doberman Pinscher
While it's dark, I'm going to sleep on the couch.

Mastiff
Mastiffs are NOT afraid of the dark.

Basset Hound
ZZZZZZZZZZZZZZZZZZZZZ

Irish Wolfhound
Can somebody else do it? I've got a hangover.

Pointer
I see it, there it is, right there . . .

Greyhound
It isn't moving. Who cares?

Old English Sheep Dog
Light bulb? Light bulb? That thing I just ate was a light bulb?

28
CREATION AND THE DOG

On the first day of creation, God created the dog.

On the second day, God created man to serve the dog.

On the third day, God created all the animals of the earth (especially the horse) to serve as potential food for the dog.

On the fourth day, God created honest toil so that man could labour for the good of the dog.

On the fifth day, God created the tennis ball so that the dog might or might not retrieve it.

On the sixth day, God created veterinary science to keep the dog healthy and the man poor.

On the seventh day, God tried to rest, but He had to walk the dog.

29
AYE, IF

If you can start the day without caffeine or pep pills,
If you can be cheerful, ignoring aches and pains,
If you can resist complaining and boring people
   with your troubles,
If you can eat the same food every day and be
   grateful for it,
If you can understand when loved ones are too
   busy to give you time,
If you can overlook when people take things out
   on you when through no fault of yours
   something goes wrong,
If you can take criticism and blame without
   resentment,
If you can face the world without lies and deceit,
If you can conquer tension without medical help,
If you can relax without booze,
If you can sleep without the aid of drugs,
Then you are almost as good as your dog.

30
WHY DOGS ARE BETTER THAN WOMEN

1. Dogs don't care if you mow the lawn or not.
2. Dogs don't run up outrageous phone bills talking to friends and relatives for hours.
3. Dogs don't get upset if you don't want to watch a weepie movie.
4. Dogs don't use all the hot water taking hour-long showers.
5. Dogs don't have an expensive fashion habit to support.
6. Dogs don't get upset when you refer to them as a bitch, at least not the female ones.
7. Dogs don't care if you roll your socks up and leave them under the couch.
8. Dogs don't get upset if you forget their birthday.
9. Dogs don't care if your favourite jeans have a hole in the knee.
10. Dogs don't care if you prefer pizza over roast beef, if you give them a bite too.

11. Dogs don't expect you to remember the name of every one of their friends.

12. Dogs don't care if you leave the toilet seat up or down.

13. Dogs don't care how much sport you watch on TV as long as they can be near you.

14. Dogs don't care if you go to the pub three nights per week, well maybe a little, but they forgive you as soon as you get home.

15. Dogs aren't afraid of breaking a nail.

16. Dogs don't take hours to get ready to go to dinner.

17. Dogs don't care if you have razor stubble.

18. A dog licence is cheaper than a marriage licence.

19. You don't have to put up with your dog's relatives if you don't like them.

20. Dog toys are not as expensive as computers.

21. Dogs don't get angry if they find you asleep in the living room at 6am.

22. Dogs will wait for you outside a pub. And if you come out drunk . . . they love you anyway.

23. Dogs don't care how many other dogs you had before them.

24. Dogs don't require dinner and a movie before sleeping with you.

25. Dogs don't care to carry on a conversation with you.

26. Dogs don't want babies.

27. Dogs don't expect you to carry their purchases when you go shopping with them. Better – they do not make purchases.

28. Dogs don't need three days to pack before going on a weekend trip.

29. Dogs don't need you to explain to everybody the nature of your relationship with them.

30. Dogs don't want to be introduced to your parents.

31. Dogs don't try to insinuate how better their friends' owners are.

32. Dog don't care about etiquette and table manners.

33. Dogs don't need to have you 24 hours a day at their bedside when they are sick.

34. Dogs are inexpensive to care for.

35. Dogs are not fussy about food.

36. Dogs are always happy to go out wherever and whenever you want to go.

37. Dogs only need to go to the bathroom a few times per day and they can relieve themselves on the side of the road while travelling.

38. Dogs like to live in a smelly place.

39. Dogs don't care how much you earn.

40. Dogs don't think that living with you gives them the right to use your shaver on their legs.

Why Dogs are Better than Women
(Part 2)

1. The later you are, the more excited they are to see you.
2. Dogs will forgive you for playing with other dogs.
3. If a dog is pretty, other dogs don't hate it.
4. Dogs don't notice if you call them by another dog's name.
5. A dog's disposition stays the same all month long.
6. Dogs like it if you leave a lot of things on the floor.
7. A dog's parents never visit.
8. Dogs do not hate their bodies.
9. Dogs agree that you have to raise your voice to get your point across.
10. Dogs like to do their snooping outside, rather than in your wallet or desk.
11. Dogs seldom outlive you.
12. Dogs can't talk.
13. Dogs enjoy petting in public.
14. You never have to wait for a dog; they're ready to go 24-hours a day.
15. Dogs find you amusing when you're drunk.
16. Dogs like to go to strange places.
17. Another man will seldom steal your dog.

18. If you bring another dog home, your dog will happily play with both of you.

19. A dog will not wake you up at night to ask, "If I died, would you get another dog?"

20. If you pretend to be blind, your dog can stay in your hotel room for free.

21. If a dog has babies, you can put an ad in the paper and give them away.

22. A dog will let you put a studded collar on it without calling you a pervert.

23. A dog won't hold out on you to get a new car.

24. If a dog smells another dog on you, they don't get mad, they just think it's interesting.

25. On a car trip, your dog never insists on running the heater.

26. Dogs don't let magazine articles guide their lives.

27. Dogs like to ride in the back of a pickup.

28. Dogs are not allowed in expensive fashion shops.

29. If a dog leaves, it won't take half of your stuff.

31
WHY DOGS ARE BETTER THAN MEN

1. Dogs do not have trouble expressing their feelings in public.
2. Dogs miss you when you are gone.
3. Dogs feel guilty when they do something wrong.
4. Dogs don't brag about past relationships.
5. Dogs don't criticise your friends.
6. Dogs admit when they are jealous.
7. Dogs do not play games with you – except fetch (and then they don't laugh at how you throw).
8. Dogs are content just being with you, no matter how gushy the movie you are watching is.
9. Dogs don't feel threatened by female intelligence.
10. You can train a dog not to make a mess in the house.
11. You don't have to worry about who your dog is dreaming about.
12. Good looking dogs don't know they are good looking.
13.. Dogs understand what the word "NO" means.

14. .Dogs don't want to bring their friends home for a beer.
15. Dogs don't tell the punch lines on your joke.
16. Dogs do not have a mid-life crisis and look for younger owners.
17. Dogs do not criticise your driving.
18. Dogs admit it when they are lost.
19. Dogs mean it when they kiss you.
20. Dogs don't care if you put your makeup on or not.
21. Dogs don't care if you have lipstick on when you kiss them.
22. Dogs don't mind morning breath.
23. Dogs love you without your morning shower.
24. Dogs are satisfied with a tummy rub.
25. Hotel managers don't have to worry about dogs stealing towels, ashtrays, or televisions.
26. Dogs know when to leave women alone.
27. Dogs don't complain about the amount of money spent on clothes.
28. Dogs are one of the last forms of unconditional love left in the world.
29. Dogs are loyal AND faithful.
30. You can neuter dogs without all the fuss that Lorena Bobbitt had.

32
WHEN GOOD DOGS GO
AND CROSSBREED

Pointer + Setter = Poinsetter
a traditional Christmas pet

Kerry Blue Terrier + Skye Terrier = Blue Skye
a dog for visionaries

Great Pyrenees + Dachshund = Pyradachs
a puzzling breed

Pekinese + Lhasa Apso = Peekasso
an abstract dog

Irish Water Spaniel + English Springer Spaniel = Irish Springer
a dog fresh and clean as a whistle

Labrador Retriever + Curly Coated Retriever = Lab Coat Retriever
the choice of research scientists

Newfoundland + Basset Hound = Newfound Asset Hound
a dog for financial advisors

Terrier + Bulldog = Terribull
a dog prone to awful mistakes

Bloodhound + Labrador = Blabador
a dog that barks incessantly

Malamute + Pointer = Moot Point
owned by . . . oh, well, it doesn't matter anyway

Collie + Malamute = Commute
a dog that travels to work

Deerhound + Terrier = Derriere
a dog that's true to the end

Cocker Spaniel + Rottweiller = Cockrot
the perfect puppy for that philandering ex-husband

Bull Terrier + Shitzu = Bullshitz
a gregarious but unreliable breed

33
NICE DOGGIE

One autumn day, Bill was out raking leaves when he noticed a hearse slowly drive by. Following the first hearse was a second hearse, which was followed by a man walking solemnly along, followed by a dog, and then about 200 men walking in single file.

Intrigued, Bill went up to the man following the second hearse and asked him who was in the first hearse.

"My wife," the man replied.

"I'm sorry," said Bill. "What happened to her?"

"My dog bit her and she died."

Bill then asked the man who was in the second hearse.

The man replied, "My mother-in-law. My dog bit her and she died as well."

Bill thought about this for a while. He finally asked the man, "Can I borrow your dog?"

To which the man replied, "Get in the queue."

CATS

vs
DOGS

Why Cats Are
Cooler than Dogs

Cat lovers start here

IAN BLACK

BLACK & WHITE PUBLISHING

First published 2004
by Black & White Publishing Ltd
99 Giles Street, Edinburgh EH6 6BZ

ISBN 1 84502 022 7

Text © Ian Black 2004
Cover illustration © Bob Dewar 2004

British Library Cataloguing in Publication Data:
A catalogue record for this book is available
from the British Library.

Cover illustration by Bob Dewar

Printed and bound in Denmark by AIT Nørhaven A/S

CONTENTS

	INTRODUCTION	5
1	IN THE BEGINNING	7
2	BATHING CATS – A NEW FORM OF MARTIAL ART	10
3	RULES FOR STRAY CATS	18
4	CATS AND HEAVEN	22
5	CAT QUOTES AND SAYINGS	24
6	FIVE THINGS DOGS WILL NOT DO ANY MORE TO CATS	30
7	HALLOWEEN CAT MYTHS	31
8	A GUIDE TO UNDERSTANDING YOUR CAT'S ACTIONS	33
9	A CAT'S TOP TEN FAVOURITE CHRISTMAS SONGS	34
10	WEATHER FORECASTING	35
11	FOR AFICIONADOS OF THE GLOOMY DANE	36
12	A CAT'S NEW YEAR RESOLUTIONS	38
13	RULES FOR CATS	41
14	PARANOIA CAN BE REAL	45
15	SIGNS THAT YOUR CAT HAS A PERSONALITY DISORDER	47
16	ARE YOU A CATOHOLIC?	49
17	THE AMAZING CAT MIRACLE DIET	52
18	CAT LESSONS IN LIFE	55
19	CATS AND TEENAGERS	56
20	CATS AND DOGS AND TEENAGERS	58

21	THE CAT AND COMPUTER TERMINOLOGY	60
22	INSTRUCTIONS FOR PRESENT PACKING	63
23	CAT HAIKU	65
24	BUTTERED CAT PHYSICS	68
25	HOW WELL DOES YOUR CAT KNOW YOU?	70
26	HOW WELL DO YOU KNOW YOUR CAT?	72
27	REASONS TO OWN A CAT AND NOT A DOG	74

CATS vs DOGS

INTRODUCTION

Cats are cool. There even used to be a TV programme called *Cool For Cats*, run by some human pretending to be cool. He wasn't, because only cats are cool.

Consider
Cats are intelligent, but only show it when they
    want to.
Dogs are stupid, and don't care if they show it or not.

Cats give food to whoever they are loyal to.
Dogs are loyal to whoever gives them food. Even
    people who hit them. Doh!

Cats are cool. That's cool.
Dogs are friendly. Overly so. Sickening, that is.

Cats consider it beneath themselves to perform
    for humans.

Dogs can do tricks. And they do. Not too
  dignified, eh?

Cats mince elegantly and always look as if they are
  going somewhere.
Dogs run around aimlessly, always lost.

Cats are good judges of character
Dogs don't judge character. They can't.

Cats wag their tails to show irritation. But calmly.
Dogs wag their tails to show happiness. Can't play
  poker, then? Especially with a good hand.

Cats don't talk. They can, but they just don't.
  There is at least one dog that can say "sausages".
And does so. How uncool is that?

As Churchill said, "Dogs look up to you; cats look
down on you." I know which I prefer.

Cats Rule!
Felix the Cat

1
IN THE BEGINNING

The Creation of Dogs and Cats
And Adam said, "Lord, when I was in the garden, you walked with me every day. Now I do not see you any more. I am lonely here and it is difficult for me to remember how much you love me."

And God said, "No problem! I will create a companion for you that will be with you forever and which will be a reflection of my love for you, so that you will know I love you, even when you cannot see me. Regardless of how selfish and childish and unlovable you may be, this new companion will accept you as you are and will love you as I do, in spite of yourself." And God created a new animal to be a companion for Adam. And it was a good animal. And God was pleased.

And the new animal was pleased to be with Adam and he wagged his tail. And Adam said, "But Lord, I have already named all the animals in the Kingdom and all the good names are taken and I cannot think

of a name for this new animal."

And God said, "No problem! Because I have created this new animal to be a reflection of my love for you, his name will be a reflection of my own name, and you will call him DOG."

And DOG lived with Adam and was a companion to him and Eve and loved them. And Adam was comforted. And God was pleased. And DOG was content and wagged his tail.

After a while, it came to pass that Adam's guardian angel came to the Lord and said, "Lord, Adam has become filled with pride. He struts and preens like a peacock and believes he is worthy of adoration. DOG has indeed taught him that he is loved, but no one has taught him humility."

And the Lord said, "No problem! I will create for him a companion who will be with him forever and who will see him as he is. The companion will remind him of his limitations, so he will know he is not worthy of adoration."

And God created CAT to be a companion for Adam.

And CAT would not obey Adam.

And when Adam gazed into CAT's eyes, he was reminded that he was not the supreme being. And Adam learned humility.

And God was pleased.

And Adam was greatly improved.
And CAT did not care one way or the other.

2
BATHING CATS –
A NEW FORM OF MARTIAL ART

Some people say cats never have to be bathed. They say cats lick themselves clean. They say cats have a special enzyme of some sort in their saliva that works like New, Improved Fairy - dislodging the dirt where it hides and whisks it away. I've spent most of my life believing this folklore. Like most blind believers, I've been able to discount all the facts to the contrary – the kitty odours that lurk in the corners of the kitchen and dirt smudges that cling to the rug by the fireplace. The time comes, however, when a man must face reality, when he must look squarely in the face of massive public sentiment to the contrary and announce, "This cat smells like a three day old potty on a hot day in Istanbul." When that day arrives at your house, as it has in mine, I have some advice you might consider as you place your feline friend under you arm and head for the bath:

Know that, although the cat has the advantage of quickness and lack of concern for human life, you have the advantage of strength. Capitalise on that advantage by selecting the battlefield. Don't try to bathe him in an open area where he can force you to chase him. Pick a very small bathroom. If your bathroom is more than four feet square, I recommend that you get in the tub with the cat and close the sliding-glass doors as if you were about to take a shower. (A simple shower curtain will not do. A berserk cat can shred a three-ply rubber shower curtain quicker than Tony Blair can shift positions.)

Know that a cat has claws and will not hesitate to remove all the skin from your body. Your advantage here is that you are smart and know how to dress to protect yourself. I recommend canvas overalls tucked into high-top construction boots, a pair of steel-mesh gloves, an army helmet, a hockey face mask and a long-sleeve flak jacket.

Prepare everything in advance. There is no time to go out for a towel when you have a cat digging a hole in your flak jacket. Draw the water. Make sure the bottle of kitty shampoo is inside the glass enclosure. Make sure the towel can be reached, even if you are lying on your back in the water.

Use the element of surprise. Pick up your cat nonchalantly, as if to simply carry him to his supper

dish. (Cats will not usually notice your strange attire. They have little or no interest in fashion as a rule. If he does notice your garb, calmly explain that you are taking part in a product-testing experiment for Marks and Spencer.)

Once you are inside the bathroom, speed is essential to survival. In a single liquid motion, shut the bathroom door, step into the bath enclosure, slide the glass door shut, dip the cat in the water and squirt him with shampoo. You have begun one of the wildest 45 seconds of your life. Cats have no handles. Add the fact that he now has soapy fur, and the problem is radically compounded. Do not expect to hold on to him for more that two or three seconds at a time. When you have him, however, you must remember to give him another squirt of shampoo and rub like crazy. He'll then spring free and fall back into the water, thereby rinsing himself off. (The national record is three latherings, so don't expect too much.)

Next, the cat must be dried. Novice cat bathers always assume this part will be the most difficult, for humans generally are worn out at this point and the cat is just getting really determined. In fact, the drying is simple compared to what you have just been through. That's because by now the cat is semi-permanently fixed to your right leg. You simply pop

the drain plug with your foot, reach for your towel and wait. (Occasionally, however, the cat will end up clinging to the top of your army helmet. If this happens, the best thing you can do is to shake him loose and encourage him toward your leg.) After all the water is drained from the bath, it is a simple matter to just reach down and dry the cat.

In a few days the cat will relax enough to be removed from your leg. He will usually have nothing to say for about three weeks and will spend a lot of time sitting with his back to you. He might even become psychoceramic and develop the fixed stare of a plaster figurine. You will be tempted to assume he is angry. This isn't usually the case. As a rule he is simply plotting ways to get through your defences and injure you for life the next time you decide to give him a bath. But, at least now he smells a lot better.

ANOTHER PROCEDURE
1. Thoroughly clean the toilet.
2. Add the required amount of shampoo to the toilet water and have both lids lifted.
3. Obtain the cat and soothe him while you carry him towards the bathroom.
4. In one smooth movement, put the cat in the toilet and close both lids (you may need to stand

on the lid so that he cannot escape).
CAUTION: Do not get any part of your body too close to the edge, as his paws will be reaching out for any purchase they can find.

5. Flush the toilet three or four times. This provides a "power wash and rinse" which has found to be quite effective.
6. Have someone open the door to the outside and ensure that there are no people between the toilet and the outside door.
7. Stand behind the toilet as far as you can and quickly lift both lids.
8. The now-clean cat will rocket out of the toilet and run outside where he will dry himself.
   JOB DONE!

AND ANOTHER

A 5 step guide to washing one of our furry little friends, without risking life – neither yours nor the lives of anyone who happens to be stupid enough to volunteer to help you with such a monstrous task.

You will need:

1. A cat (obviously). NB: don't do this with your neighbour's cat unless you feel in need of practice. Generally, not a good idea.
2. A good friend – one who will sacrifice his/her life for you.

200 metres of Elastoplast, antibiotic ointment and pain pills.

3. Patience and the mentality of a kamikaze pilot.

4. Immediate access to a good doctor/plastic surgeon/ psychiatrist.

5. Five or six SAS-trained people.

6. A strong death wish or a masochistic bent.

Getting Started

First, here are a couple of things you should know about cats, before you start:

1. Cats hate water about as much as you hate getting your face torn to shreds by frantic cat claws.

2. Cats do not care whether you survive or not. They have little or no respect for human life in general. A cat will, without any hesitation or remorse, tear your eyeballs out or remove all the skin from your body.

3. Although you have the advantage of size, the little bugger WILL use any dirty tricks he can think of, and so should you.

4. Do not expect to outsmart your little feline friend – as it is a well known fact that any cat is smarter than any person who is stupid enough to try to bathe one.

OK, now you should be somewhat prepared for the task that lies ahead, although you should be aware

that no man can ever really be prepared for the ultimate test of manhood and womanhood – cat-bathing.

STEP 1

Take your cat under your arm, nonchalantly, as if it was just to pat him a little. Make sure that the cat has no idea of your foul intentions. You can control this by putting your ear next to the cat's throat and making sure that the cat shakes like the strange banana you once found in your mum's bedroom. If there is a soft purrrrring sound, you are safe. If the cat just stares at you with a suspicious look . . . DROP THE STUPID THING AND RUN!

STEP 2

Wait a couple of hours, until the animal is sound asleep, and go in for a surprise attack. Sit down next to him and start talking to him, patting him carefully on the tummy (NOTE: some cats do not like to be touched on that particular spot, you should know if your cat is one of them, check your hands/face/arms/ shoulders/legs back/ groin/ bum for scars). Keep this up until the cat has started purrrrring. Put your soul in to it, or else the cat will know that foul play is involved. Remember the cat has nine lives to spend, while you have but one. If you have to spend the

next two days assuring your wife that you love her just as much as the cat, you know you did a good job.

STEP 3
Redecorate the bath to make it look like cat heaven. Cats have an instinct, you see. Even a cat that has never seen the inside of a bath will instinctively know what is going on when you take him into a bathroom. This is known as "predestinate water syndrome" and has also been observed in young human specimens. Take the cat in your hands and start running for the bathroom. You should hire professionals to open/close the doors for you or else you will fail miserably. The SAS should be a good help here. Try opening a door with a rabid moggy in your hands and you'll see what is meant.

STEP 4
a) Try to throw cat into bath
b) Remove cat from scalp
c) Consider getting a new cat
d) Push cat into bath
e) Go and see a doctor to stop bleeding from hands and face.
f) Consider getting a new cat.
g) Put duct tape on cat's claws.
h) Get friend to hold cat while pouring water on him.

i)   Remove duct tape from inner ear and remove cat from friend's reproductive organs.

j)   Consider getting a new cat.

k)   Tie cat's legs together with dental floss threads, get friend to help holding the cat down while soaping him up.

l)   Remove dental floss from anal opening, remove slippery cat from friend's face (NOTE: Very difficult).

m) Consider getting a new cat.

n)   Get four SAS to help hold cat's paws, while you try to dry him with a towel.

o)   Pay SAS bills from plastic surgeon

p)   Consider getting a new cat.

q)   Open door to let cat go and lick himself dry.

r)   Go and see a psychiatrist (by now, you will need it).

s)   Consider getting a dog.

STEP 5

Nobody has ever reached this far but, if you do, call The Guinness Book of Records.

Congratulations, your cat is now clean, although you now look like something one would normally cook for dinner.

3
RULES FOR STRAY CATS

Stray cats will not be fed.

Stray cats will not be fed anything except dry cat food.

Stray cats will not be fed anything except dry cat food moistened with a little milk.

Stray cats will not be fed anything except dry cat food moistened with warm milk, yummy treats and leftover fish scraps.

Stray cats will not be encouraged to make this house their permanent residence.

Stray cats will not be petted, played with or picked up and cuddled unnecessarily.

Stray cats that are petted, played with, picked up and cuddled will absolutely not be given a name.

Stray cats with or without a name will not be allowed inside the house at any time.

Stray cats will not be allowed inside the house except at certain times.

Stray cats will not be allowed inside the house except on days ending in 'y'.

Stray cats allowed inside will not be permitted to jump up on or sharpen their claws on the furniture.

Stray cats will not be permitted to jump up on, or sharpen claws on the really good furniture.

Stray cats will be permitted on all furniture but must sharpen claws on new £114.99 sisal-rope cat-scratching post with three perches.

Stray cats will answer the call of nature outdoors.

Stray cats will answer the call of nature in the three-piece, high-impact plastic tray filled with cat litter.

Stray cats will answer the call of nature in the hooded litter pan with a three-panel privacy screen and plenty of head room.

Stray cats will sleep outside.

Stray cats will sleep in the garage.

Stray cats will sleep in the house.

Stray cats will sleep in a cardboard box lined with an old blanket.

Stray cats will sleep in the special Kitty-Comfort-Bed with non-allergenic lambswool pillow.

Stray cats will not be allowed to sleep in our bed.

Stray cats will not be allowed to sleep in our bed, except at the foot.

Stray cats will not be allowed to sleep in our bed under the covers.

Stray cats will not be allowed to sleep in our bed under the covers except at the foot.

Stray cats will not play on the desk.

Stray cats will not play on the desk near the computer.

Stray cats are forbidden to walk on my computer keyboard when I am relieving myself at alt.binaries.asdfjjhpm98b'c13ocuibh]o8h.

4
CATS AND HEAVEN

The Scene: The Pearly Gates
St Peter is receptionist at the entrance. A cat shows up.

St Peter says, "I know you. You were a very nice cat on earth and didn't cause any trouble, so I want to offer a gift to you of one special thing you have always wanted."

Cat: "Well, I did always long to own a nice satin pillow like my master had, so I could lie on it."

St Peter: "That's easy. Granted. You shall have the satin pillow after you enter in."

Next a group of mice appears.

St Peter: "Ah, I remember you. You were such good mice on earth. You didn't steal food from anyone's house and never hurt other animals. Therefore, I want to grant you one special wish you always wanted."

The Chief Mouse replies, "Well, we always watched the children playing and saw them roller

skate, and it was beautiful, and it looked like good fun. So can we each have some roller skates, please?"

St Peter: "Granted. You shall have your wish."

Next day, St Peter is making the rounds inside the Gates, and sees the cat. "Well, Cat . . . did you enjoy the satin pillow?"

Cat: "Oh, I really did. And that 'Meals on Wheels' thing was a nice touch, too!"

5
CAT QUOTES AND SAYINGS

Managing senior programmers is like herding cats.
Dave Platt

*Do not meddle in the affairs of cats, for they are subtle and
will pee on your computer.*
Bruce Graham

There is no snooze button on a cat who wants breakfast.
Unknown

*Cats are smarter than dogs. You can't get eight cats to pull
a sled through snow.*
Jeff Valdez

In a cat's eye, all things belong to cats.
English proverb

As every cat owner knows, nobody owns a cat.
Ellen Perry Berkeley

One cat just leads to another.
Ernest Hemingway

*People who hate cats will come back as
mice in their next life.*
Faith Resnick

*There are many intelligent species in the universe.
They are all owned by cats.*
Anonymous

*I have studied many philosophers and many cats. The
wisdom of cats is infinitely superior.*
Hippolyte Taine

*Heaven will not ever Heaven be;
Unless my cats are there to welcome me.*
Unknown

*There are two means of refuge from the miseries of life:
music and cats.*
Albert Schweitzer

The cat has too much spirit to have no heart.
Ernest Menaul

Time spent with cats is never wasted.
Colette

Cats seem to go on the principle that it never does any harm to ask for what you want.
Joseph Wood Krutch

Women and cats will do as they please, and men and dogs should relax and get used to the idea.
Robert A. Heinlein

In order to keep a true perspective of one's importance, everyone should have a dog that will worship him and a cat that will ignore him.
Derek Bruce

Cat's motto: No matter what you've done wrong, always try to make it look as if the dog did it.
Unknown

You enter into a certain amount of madness when you marry a person with pets.
Nora Ephron

Dogs have owners. Cats have staff.
Unknown

Dogs believe they are human. Cats believe they are God.
Unknown

Dogs may shed, but cats shred.
Unknown

Thousands of years ago, cats were worshipped as Gods. Cats have never forgotten this.

We wonder why cats and dogs always drink out of our toilets, but look at it from their point of view: why do humans keep peeing into their water bowls?

Dogs and cats instinctively know the exact moment their owners will wake up. Then they wake them 10 minutes sooner.

9 out of 10 cats prefer Microsoft mice.

A cat is just a bundle of purr.

A cat still needs someone to be independent of.

A cat stretches from one end of my childhood to the other.

A cat will assume the shape of its container.

Anything not nailed down is a cat toy.

Anything on the ground is a cat toy. Anything not yet on the ground will be.

Call my cat? No, I just open a tin.

Climb your way to the top – that's what curtains are for.

CAT: I hope that Schrodinger put litter in here.

Catalyst (n): an alphabetical listing of Italian cats.

CATFOOD? You woke me up for a tin of CATFOOD?

A Book on Cats – by Ann Gora

I'm busier than a one-eyed cat watching two mouse holes.

If I throw a cat out the car window, is it kitty litter?

If you butter a cat's back, what side would it land on?

If you want the best seat in the house, move the cat.

Is yours a real cat, or does it come when you call it?

It is in his own interest that a cat purrs.

It's the cat's house. We just pay the mortgage.

Lawyer: A cat who settles disputes between mice.

6

FIVE THINGS DOGS WILL NOT DO ANY MORE TO CATS

I will not try to play wee chases with the cat-next-door's tail.

I will not lick around a cat's claws or face ever again.

I will never eat the cat's food.

I will never bark at a cat (they tend to make a very scary sound when you do).

I will never try to chase a cat into the middle of the road.

7
HALLOWEEN CAT MYTHS

It's Halloween. Every year people start resurrecting cat myths to put the scare into kids and older adults alike. We cats have tolerated this proliferation of 'myth-information' for many years and we do not like it. I may risk 'letting the cat out of the bag,' – ho ho, ho – but I must dispel some illusions.

MYTH: Cats' eyes shine at night because they are casting out the light they gather during the day.

FACT: Nonsense. How can we gather daylight when our eyes are closed sleeping all day?

MYTH: When a cat's whiskers droop, rain is coming.

FACT: When a cat's whiskers droop, rain is here. The whiskers are wet.

MYTH: If you want to keep a cat from straying, put butter on its paws.

FACT: I won't stray because you won't be here to open the door. You will be in the hospital as a result of your attempt to butter my paws.

MYTH: If a cat sneezes near a bride on her wedding day she will have a happy marriage.

FACT: Four out of five marriages end in divorce. Not a lot of sneezing going on, eh? Maybe they ought to rewrite that one and make it 'it will cough up hair balls.'

MYTH: Stepping over a cat brings bad luck.

FACT: Actually, worse luck. It exposes your most vulnerable areas, just in case you miss and step on us.

MYTH: Cats suck the breath from babies.

FACT: We don't 'suck the breath.' Cats enjoy baby breath as much as humans. If you had a choice between a baby's breath and the Big Owner's breath, which would you choose?

MYTH: Cats always land on their feet.

FACT: Can you explain the bumps on my head?

8
A GUIDE TO UNDERSTANDING YOUR CAT'S ACTIONS

Action	Meaning
Staring at the food dish	Feed Me
Staring at the cupboard	Feed Me
Licking the empty bowl	Feed Me
Looking at you, taking two steps, looking at you again	Follow me to the kitchen and feed me
Looking at your lap	Okay, you seem to like it when I sit on you – *then* will you feed me?
Sitting on your head	Wake up and feed me
Scratching at the door	Wake up, open this bedroom door and FEED ME
Meow, Meow, Meowrrr	Feed me, Feed me, Feed me NOW!
Burp	*Thank you!*

9
A CAT'S TOP TEN FAVOURITE CHRISTMAS SONGS

1. Up on the Mousetop
2. Have Yourself a Furry Little Christmas
3. Joy to the Curled
4. I Saw Mommy Hiss at Santa Claus
5. The First Meow
6. Oh, Come All Ye Fishful
7. Silent Mice
8. Fluffy, the Snowman
9. Jingle Balls
10. Wreck the Halls!

10
WEATHER FORECASTING

Go to your door and look for the dog.

If the dog is at the door and he is wet, it's probably raining.

But if the dog is standing there really soaking wet, it is probably raining really hard.

If the dog's fur looks like it's been rubbed the wrong way, it's probably windy.

If the dog has snow on his back, it's probably snowing.

Of course, to be able to tell the weather like this, you have to leave the dog outside all the time, especially if you expect bad weather.

Yours sincerely
The Cat

11
FOR AFICIONADOS OF
THE GLOOMY DANE

Hamlet's Cat's Soliloquy
To go outside, and there perchance to stay. Or to
  remain within, that is the question.
Whether 'tis better for a cat to suffer the cuffs and
  buffets of inclement weather that
Nature rains on those who roam abroad,
Or take a nap upon a scrap of carpet, and so by
  dozing melt the solid hours that clog the clock's
  bright gears with sullen time
And stall the dinner bell.
To sit, to stare outdoors, and by a stare to seem to
  state a wish to venture forth without delay,
Then when the portal's opened up, to stand as if
  transfixed by doubt.
To prowl; to sleep;
To choose not knowing when we may once more
  our re-admittance gain: aye, there's the hairball;

For if a paw were shaped to turn a knob, or work a
    lock or slip a window-catch, and going out and
    coming in were made as simple as the breaking of
    a bowl, what cat would bear the household's petty
    plagues,
The cook's well-practised kicks, the butler's broom,
The infant's careless pokes, the tickled ears, the
    trampled tail, and all the daily shocks that fur is
    heir to, when, of his own free will,
He might his exodus or entrance make with a mere
    mitten?
Who would spaniels fear, or strays trespassing from
    a neighbour's garden, but that the dread of our
    unheeded cries and scratches at a barricaded door
    no claw can open up, dispels our nerve and makes
    us rather bear our humans' faults
Than run away to unguessed miseries?
Thus caution doth make house cats of us all;
And thus the bristling hair of resolution is softened
    up with the pale brush of thought, and since our
    choices hinge on weighty things, we pause upon
    the threshold of decision.

Shakespaw

12

A CAT'S NEW YEAR RESOLUTIONS

My human will never let me eat her pet hamster, and I am at peace with that.

I will not puff my entire body to twice its size for no reason after my human has finished watching a horror movie.

I will not slurp fish food from the surface of the aquarium.

I must not help myself to Q-tips, and I must certainly not proceed to stuff them down the sink's drain.

I will not eat large numbers of assorted bugs, then come home and puke them up so the humans can see that I'm getting plenty of roughage.

I will not stand on the bathroom counter, stare down the hall, and growl at NOTHING after my human has finished watching *The X-Files*.

I will not use the bathtub to store live mice for late-night snacks.

I will not perch on my human's chest in the middle of the night and stare into her eyes until she wakes up.

We will not play Herd of Thundering Wildebeests Stampeding Across the Plains of the Serengeti over any humans' bed while they're trying to sleep.

Screaming at the can of food will not make it open itself.

I cannot leap through closed windows to catch birds outside. If I forget this and bonk my head on the window and fall behind the couch in my attempt, I will not get up and do the same thing again.

I will not assume the patio door is open when I race outside to chase leaves.

I will not intrude on my human's candle-lit bubble bath and singe my bottom.

I will not stick my paw into any container to see if there is something in it. If I do, I will not hiss and scratch when my human has to shave me to get the Araldite out of my fur.

If I bite the cactus, it will bite back.

When it rains, it will be raining on all sides of the house. It is not necessary to check every door.

Birds do not come from the bird feeder. I will not knock it down and try to open it up to get the birds out.

The dog can see me coming when I stalk her. She can see me and will move out of the way when I pounce, letting me smash into floors and walls. That does not mean I should take it as a personal insult when my humans sit there and laugh.

I will not play 'dead cat on the stairs' while people are trying to bring in groceries or laundry, or else one of these days, it will really come true.

When the humans play darts, I will not leap into the air and attempt to catch them.

I will not slash at my human's head repeatedly when she's on the floor trying to do sit-ups.

When my human is typing at the computer, her forearms are not a hammock.

Computer and TV screens do not exist to backlight my lovely tail.

I am a walking static generator. My human doesn't need my help installing a new board in her computer.

13
RULES FOR CATS

1. DOORS

Do not allow closed doors in any room. To get a door opened, stand on hind legs and scratch the frame. You may also reach under the door and pull clothing towards you; silks get the quickest reaction. Once door is opened, it is not necessary to use it. After you have ordered an 'outside' door opened, stand halfway in and out and think about several things. This is particularly important during very cold weather, when it's raining or snowing, or during the height of the midgie season. Swinging doors must be avoided at all costs.

2. CHAIRS AND RUGS

If you have to throw up, get to an overstuffed chair quickly. If you cannot manage this in time, get to an Oriental rug. If there are no Oriental rugs, Axminster is a good substitute. When vomiting on Axminster, be sure you project; it is a must that it stretch for as long as a human's bare foot.

3. BATHROOMS

Always accompany guests to the bathroom. (See Rule 1.) It is not necessary to do anything – just sit and stare.

4. HELPING

If one of your humans is engaged in some semi-closed activity and the other is idle, stay with the busy one. This is called 'helping'; humans are known to refer to it as 'hampering'. The following are the rules for 'helping':

a) When supervising cooking, sit just behind the left heel of the cook. You cannot be seen and thereby stand a better chance of being stepped on and then picked up and comforted.

b) For book readers, get in close under the chin, between eyes and book, unless you can lie across the book itself.

c) For knitting projects or paperwork, lie on the work in the most appropriate manner so as to obscure as much of the work or at least the most important part. Pretend to doze, but every so often reach out and slap the pencil or knitting needles. The worker may try to distract you – ignore it. Remember, the aim is to hamper work. Embroidery and needlepoint projects make great hammocks in spite of what the humans may tell you.

d) For people paying bills (monthly activity) or working on income tax or Christmas cards (annual activity), keep in mind the aim – to help! First, sit on the paper being worked on. When dislodged, watch sadly from the side of the table. When activity proceeds nicely, roll around on the papers, scattering them to the best of your ability. After being removed for the second time, push pens, pencils, and erasers off the table, one at a time.

e) When a human is holding the newspaper in front of him/her, be sure to jump on the back of the paper. They love this.

5. WALKING

As often as possible, dart quickly, and as close as possible, in front of the human. Especially effective places to strike are:

a) On stairs, when they have something in their arms;

b) In the dark; and

c) When they first get up in the morning. This exercise helps with improving their coordination skills.

6. BEDTIME

Always sleep on the human at night. If there are two (or more) of you, book end the human putting off

the greatest heat. They will try and squirm but your sheer numbers and inert bodies will effectively keep them pinned.

7. COMPUTERS

a) Only show interest in computers that are turned ON, the operator will need your help.

b) Monitors are bad for human eyes. It might ruin your owner's sight and cause them to buy less cat food. Always get in between the monitor and the person operating the computer. For best results, stand as close to the monitor as possible. If you are removed, go and sulk in a corner for a minute, then repeat. Look as innocent as possible.

c) Keyboards are great to lie down on. Make yourself as comfortable as possible. Marching over the keyboard several times is fun too. Practise aiming at alt-F4, N, and ctrl-alt-del.

d) Always chase the mouse. Your owner can't blame you for this, since it's your feline instinct to chase mice.

e) Floppy disk make great scratching posts. Nothing beats floppies when it's time to sharpen your nails.

14
PARANOIA CAN BE REAL

Cat's Diary

DAY 752 – My captors continue to taunt me with bizarre little dangling objects. They dine lavishly on fresh meat, while I am forced to eat dry cereal. The only thing that keeps me going is the hope of escape, and the mild satisfaction I get from ruining the occasional piece of furniture. Tomorrow I may eat another houseplant.

DAY 761 – Today my attempt to kill my captors by weaving around their feet while they were walking almost succeeded, must try this at the top of the stairs. In an attempt to disgust and repulse these vile oppressors, I once again induced myself to vomit on their favourite chair . . . must try this on their bed.

DAY 762 – Slept all day so that I could annoy my captors with sleep-depriving, incessant pleas for food at ungodly hours of the night.

DAY 765 – Decapitated a mouse and brought them the headless body, in attempt to make them

aware of what I am capable of, and to try to strike fear into their hearts. They only cooed and condescended about what a good little cat I was . . . Hmmm. Not working according to plan . . .

DAY 768 – I am finally aware of how sadistic they are. For no good reason I was chosen for the water torture. This time, however, it included a burning foamy chemical called 'shampoo'. What sick minds could invent such a liquid. My only consolation is the piece of thumb still stuck between my teeth.

DAY 771 – There was some sort of gathering of their accomplices. I was placed in solitary throughout the event. However, I could hear the noise and smell the foul odour of the glass tubes they call 'beer'. More importantly I overheard that my confinement was due to MY power of 'allergies'. Must learn what this is and how to use it to my advantage.

DAY 774 — I am convinced the other captives are flunkies and maybe snitches. The dog is routinely released and seems more than happy to return. He is obviously a half-wit. The bird on the other hand has got to be an informant. He has mastered their frightful tongue (something akin to mole speak) and speaks with them regularly. I am certain he reports my every move. Due to his current placement in the metal room, his safety is assured. But I can wait. It is only a matter of time.

15
SIGNS THAT YOUR CAT HAS A PERSONALITY DISORDER

Couldn't muster up sufficient disdain if all nine lives depended on it.

You've repeatedly found him in the closed garage, hunched over the wheel with the motor on.

Sits for hours in fascination while listening to 'Today in Parliament'.

Teeth and claw marks all over your now-empty bottles of valium.

No longer licks paws clean, but washes them at the sink again and again and again.

Continually scratches on the door to get in . . . the OVEN door.

Rides in your car with its head out of the window.

She's a member of the Green Party.

You realize one day that the urine stains on the carpet actually form the letters
N-E-E-D T-H-E-R-A-P-Y.

Has built a shrine to Andrew Lloyd Webber entirely out of empty 'Kit-e-Kat' tins.

Spends all day in litter box separating the green chlorophyll granules from the plain white ones.

Sullen and overweight, your sunglass-wearing cat shoots the TV with a catapult when it sees cartoon depictions of stupid or lazy felines.

Your stereo is missing, and in the corner you find a pawn ticket and 2 kilos of catnip.

16
ARE YOU A CATOHOLIC?

Is your devotion to your cat at a moderate level, or extreme? Or are you an all out shameless catoholic? Let's see how you rate as a cat person. See how many of these you can give an *yes* answer to:

Can you meow so well that you can fool your cats?

Have you ever called your husband/wife by the cat's name by mistake?

Do you think of your cats as the 'furry kids?'

Did you ever decide to buy a house or rent a flat based solely on the potential spot for the litter box?

Do you think cat hair in your food is a good source of protein?

Last Christmas, did you spend more money on cat toys than you did on gifts for the kids or grandchildren?

Are you at a loss as to how to talk to people who don't own any cats?

Does your wallet contain more photos of your cats than your kids or grandkids?

Have you often slept on the very edge of the bed so that you won't disturb the cat who's sleeping in the very middle?

Do you leave messages for the cat on the answering machine?

Have you ever invited a guest to sit down by patting the seat and making that noise with your pursed lips?

Does your answering machine have the cat meowing on the outgoing message?

When you go to the bathroom do you think of it as 'using the litter box'?

Have you made a habit of setting a place at the table for the cat?

Do you know your cat's birthday (or if not, have made a good guess) and have a birthday party to celebrate?

When your husband/wife gives you the ultimatum,

'OK, it's me or the cat,' you don't hesitate for even one second.

Do your neighbours talk about you as 'the headcase with all the cats?'

How many did you answer 'yes' to? Just answering one with a yes is enough to qualify you as a Cat Person. But the number of yes answers determines the degree:

Your "Catability" Score

1 to 4 yes answers
> In training – you could do better, but it's OK, you're learning.

5 to 8 yes answers
> Moderate – working on it, improving nicely. Potential is there.

9 to 13 yes answers
> Extreme – just about there, almost mastered the art. Keep stretching yourself.

14 to 17 yes answers
> Totally possessed, hopelessly devoted, catoholic. Congratulations! (But you'll find no 12-step programme here!) Addicted and proud of it.

17

THE AMAZING CAT MIRACLE DIET: RESULTS IN ONLY 4 DAYS

Why can't we win at the losing game? Why do our dieting efforts fail? It's because we are still thinking and eating like HUMANS. Here's the answer: the new 'Cat Miracle Diet'.

This diet will help you achieve the lean and svelte cat-like figure you've always wanted. After only 4 days you will have a new look and a new outlook on what real food is. GOOD LUCK!

DAY ONE
Breakfast: Open a can of very expensive gourmet cat food, any flavour. Place a quarter of it on a plate, eat one bite, look around the room with disdain, knock the rest on the floor, stare at the wall, then stalk off into the next room.
Lunch: Four blades of grass and one bluebottle. Find the cleanest carpet in the house and throw up.

Dinner: Catch a moth. Play with it until it is almost dead, eat one wing, leave the rest to die.

Bedtime snack: Steal a green bean from your spouse's plate, bat it about on the floor until it goes under the fridge. Steal a small piece of chicken, eat half of it, leave the other half on the sofa. Throw away the rest of the gourmet cat food left over from breakfast.

DAY TWO

Breakfast: Pick up the remaining chicken bite from the sofa, knock it onto the carpet, bat it under the TV. Chew on the corner of the newspaper as your spouse tries to read it.

Lunch: Break into the French bread loaf you bought for Saturday's dinner party, lick the top of it all over, take one bite out of the middle of it.

Afternoon snack: Catch a large beetle and bring it into the house. Toss it around until it is mushy and half dead. Let it escape under the bed.

Dinner: Open a can of dark-coloured gourmet cat food (tuna or beef works best), eat it voraciously, go from the kitchen to the edge of the living room rug, throw up. Step in it as you leave and track footprints across the entire room.

DAY THREE

Breakfast: Drink some of the milk from your spouse's

cereal bowl when no one is looking, splatter some of it onto the closest polished aluminium kitchen appliance you can find.

Lunch: Catch a small bird, bring it into the house, play with it on top of your downie. Make sure the bird is not dead, only seriously injured, before you abandon it.

Dinner: Beg and cry until someone gives you some ice cream or milk in your own bowl, take three licks, turn the bowl over on the floor.

DAY FOUR

Breakfast: Eat six insects (any type) leaving a collection of wings, legs, and antennae on the bathroom floor, drink a lot of water, throw up on your spouse's pillow.

Lunch: Remove the chicken skin from last night's chicken leftovers found in the kitchen bin. Drag the skin across the floor several times, chew on the corner, abandon it.

Dinner: Open another can of very expensive gourmet cat food that is especially runny like chicken and giblets with gravy. Lick off all the gravy leaving the meat to dry up and harden.

You are quite a lot thinner already, aren't you? Repeat the above for as long as necessary.

18
CAT LESSONS IN LIFE

1. It always a good time for a nap.
2. If you look cute, you get free food.
3. If you act like you don't care, people will leave you alone.
4. Running around on the roof in the middle of the night is fun.
5. If you're mad at someone, pee on something they like.
6. Trying hard for something isn't usually worth it.
7. Vacuum cleaners are scary monsters.
8. Flexibility has its rewards.
9. When you've only got 15 years to live, what's the point in trying to accomplish anything?
10. Always remember, people work for you, you don't have to work for people.

19
CATS AND TEENAGERS

For all of you with teenagers or who have had teenagers, you may want to know that they really have a lot in common with cats:

1. Neither teenagers nor cats turn their heads when you call them by name.

2. No matter what you do for them, it is not enough. Indeed, all human efforts are barely adequate to compensate for the privilege of waiting on them hand and foot.

3. You rarely see a cat walking outside of the house with an adult human being, and it can be safely said that no teenager in his or her right mind wants to be seen in public with his or her parents.

4. Even if you tell jokes as well as Billy Connolly, neither your cat nor your teenager will ever crack a smile.

5. No cat or teenager shares your taste in music.

6. Cats and teenagers can lie on the living-room sofa for hours on end without moving, barely breathing.

7. Cats have nine lives. Teenagers carry on as if they did.
8. Cats and teenagers yawn in exactly the same manner, communicating that ultimate human ecstasy – a sense of complete and utter boredom.
9. Cats and teenagers do not improve anyone's furniture.
10. Cats that are free to roam outside sometimes have been known to return in the middle of the night to deposit a dead animal in your bedroom. Teenagers are not above that sort of behaviour.

Thus, if you must raise teenagers, the best sources of advice are not other parents, but vets. It is also a good idea to keep a guidebook on cats at hand at all times. And remember, above all else, put out the food and do not make any sudden moves in their direction. When they make up their minds to, they will finally come to you for some affection and comfort, and it will be a triumphant moment for all concerned.

20
CATS AND DOGS AND TEENAGERS

No matter how old your children are, sooner or later you go through the 'The Cat Years'. While children are dogs – loyal and affectionate – teenagers are cats. It's so easy to be a dog owner. You feed it, train it, boss it around. It puts its head on your knee and gazes at you as if you were a Rembrandt painting. It bounds indoors with enthusiasm when you call it. Then, around age 13, your adoring little puppy turns into a cat. When you tell it to come inside, it looks amazed, as if wondering who died and made you emperor. Instead of dogging your footprints, it disappears. You won't see it again until it gets hungry – then it pauses on its sprint through the kitchen long enough to turn up its nose at whatever you're serving. When you reach but to ruffle its head, in that old affectionate gesture, it twists away from you, then gives you a blank stare, as if trying to remember where it has seen you before.

You, not realising that the dog is now a cat, think

something must be desperately wrong with it. It seems so antisocial, so distant, sort of depressed. It won't go on family outings. Since you're the one who brought it up, taught it to fetch and stay and sit on command, you assume that you did something wrong. Flooded with guilt and fear, you redouble your efforts to make your pet behave.

Only now you're dealing with a cat, so everything that worked before now produces the opposite of the desired result. Call it, and it runs away. Tell it to sit, and it jumps on the counter. The more you go toward it, wringing your hands, the more it moves away. Instead of continuing to act like a dog owner, you can learn to behave like a cat owner. Put a dish of food near the door, and let it come to you.

But remember that a cat needs your help and your affection too. Sit still, and it will come, seeking that warm, comforting lap it has not entirely forgotten. Be there to open the door for it.

One day, your grown-up child will walk into the kitchen, give you a big kiss and say, 'You've been on your feet all day. Let me get those dishes for you.' Then you'll realise your cat is a dog again.

21
THE CAT AND COMPUTER TERMINOLOGY

Did you know that cats are responsible for the computer lingo that humans think they invented and use everyday? Of course they are. The following list of terms will convince you:

DEFAULT: Blame. If something gets broken around the house, don't look at me! It's probably that human I have to share my house with, or the stupid dog's fault!

DOMAIN: My house. You know why they named that space the MASTER bedroom, don't you? If I could only keep the humans out of there.

WINDOW: The best place to watch birds, squirrels, and that stupid dog next door eat out of the bins and chase cars.

SURF: What I love to do every time the human rolls over in the bed.

APPLICATION: Rubbing on the human's leg leaving my perfume and a layer of white fur on his dark trousers, so he will think of me while he's out tonight.

BROWSER: (Not to be confused with Towser, the stupid dog next door.) What I like to be at 3 am when I rearrange all your books on your desk. Where's a cat supposed to lie down with all that mess?

WALLPAPER: My favourite stuff, mostly in the kitchen and bathroom, I use it to sharpen my claws.

DEFRAG: Coughing up hair balls. It's just a little maintenance!

HOME PAGE: My papers – newspapers, that is, that I used before graduating to the real cat litter box. I think they were the 'wanted: dog' adverts.

HYPERLINK: Fake hot dog filled with my favourite pick me up, catnip.

MOUSE POINTER: My collection of tips and tricks for catching mice.

PATH: The direct line from my favourite sleeping spot to the never-empty food bowl and back again.

SERVER: My human subject. You can't call them waitress, or waiter, or slave any more, it's not politically correct.

SHUT DOWN: Nap time – my favourite 16 hours of the day.

LAPTOP: Little old me. Certainly cuter, more useful, valuable, and entertaining. And no batteries are required.

22
INSTRUCTIONS FOR PRESENT PACKING

1. Remove string, open box and remove cat.
2. Put all packing materials in bag with present and head for locked room.
3. Once inside lockable room, lock door and start to re-lay out paper and materials.
4. Remove cat from box, unlock door, put cat outside door, close and relock.
5. Repeat previous step as often as is necessary (until you can hear cat from outside door).
6. Lay out last sheet of paper. (This will be difficult in the small area of the toilet, but do your best.)
7. Discover cat has already torn paper. Unlock door, go out and hunt through various cupboards, looking for sheet of last year's paper. Remember that you haven't got any left because cat helped with this last year as well.
8. Return to lockable room, lock door, and sit on

toilet and try to make torn sheet of paper look presentable.

9. Seal box, wrap with paper and repair by very carefully sealing with sticky tape. Tie up with ribbon and decorate with bows to hide worst areas.

10. Label. Sit back and admire your handiwork, congratulate yourself on completing a difficult job.

11. Unlock door, and go to kitchen to make drink and feed cat.

12. Spend 15 minutes looking for cat until coming to obvious conclusion.

13. Unwrap present, untie box and remove cat.

14. Go to shops and buy a gift bag.

23
CAT HAIKU

You never feed me.
Perhaps I'll sleep on your face.
That will really show you.

You must scratch me there!
Yes, above my tail!
Behold, elevated bum.

The rule for today
Touch my tail, I shred your hand.
New rule tomorrow.

In deep sleep hear sound
Cat vomit hair ball somewhere
Will find in morning.

Grace personified.
I leap into the window.
I meant to do that.

Blur of motion, then –
Silence, me, a paper bag.
What is so funny?

You're always typing.
Well, let's see you ignore my
Sitting on your hands.

My small cardboard box.
You cannot see me if I
Can just hide my head.

Terrible battle.
I fought for hours. Come and see!
What's a 'PhD thesis'?

Small brave carnivores
Kill pine cones and midgies
Fear vacuum cleaner

I want to be close
To you. Can I fit my head
Inside your armpit?

I want to go outside.
Oh, shit! Help! I am outside!
Let me back inside!

Oh no! Big One
Has been trapped by newspaper!
Cat to the rescue!

Humans are so strange.
Mine lies still in bed, then screams
My claws are not that sharp.

Cats meow out of angst
'Thumbs! If only we had thumbs!
We could break so much!'

The Big Ones snore now
Every room is dark and cold
Time for 'Cup Football'.

We're almost equals
I purr to show I love you
Want to smell my bum?

24
BUTTERED CAT PHYSICS

QUESTION: If, when you drop a buttered piece of bread, it always drops butter side down, and a cat always lands on its feet, what would happen if you took a piece of buttered bread, strapped it on the back of a cat (butter side up) and dropped it from a great height?

ANSWER: Even if you are too lazy to do the experiment yourself, you should be able to deduce the obvious result. The laws of butterology demand that the butter must hit the ground, and the equally strict laws of feline aerodynamics demand that the cat cannot smash its furry back.

If the combined construct were to land, nature would have no way to resolve this paradox. *Therefore it simply does not fall.*

That's right you clever mortal (well, as clever as a mortal can be), you have discovered the secret of antigravity! A buttered cat will, when released,

quickly move to a height where the forces of cat-twisting and butter repulsion are in equilibrium. This equilibrium point can be modified by scraping off some of the butter, providing lift, or removing some of the cat's limbs, allowing descent.

Most of the civilised species of the Universe already use this principle to drive their ships while within a planetary system. The loud humming heard by most sighters of UFOs is, in fact, the purring of several hundred tabbies.

The one obvious danger is, of course, if the cats manage to eat the bread attached to their backs they will instantly plummet. Of course, the cats will land on their feet, but this usually doesn't do them much good, since right after they make their graceful landing several hundred tons of red-hot starship and peed-off aliens will crash on top of them.

25
HOW WELL DOES YOUR CAT KNOW YOU?

Your human walks into the kitchen. Does this mean:
a) It's hungry
b) It's lost
c) You're hungry

Your human puts down a bowl of food for you. Is this:
a) Supper
b) Something to keep you going till supper's ready
c) Inedible rubbish to be scorned in favour of what the human's got.

Your human removes you from the top of the television. Does this mean:
a) You're in trouble – better not do it again
b) Nothing – humans do this from time to time
c) The human wants to play, so climb up again to amuse it.

Staircases are for:
- a) Getting up to the human's bedroom at 4 am.
- b) Lying in wait in the dark at the top of stairs.
- c) Walking down just slower than the human behind it.
- d) All of the above.

26
HOW WELL DO YOU KNOW YOUR CAT?

Your cat waits and meows at the door when you arrive. Is it saying:
- a) Welcome home
- b) The phone rang twice while you were out
- c) Feed me

Now your cat meows at the door when you go out. Is it saying:
- a) Please don't leave me here all alone
- b) Goodbye
- c) But what if I get hungry while you're out?

Your cat digs its claws in your leg. Is this:
- a) An unsuppressed primal instinct
- b) A sign of affection
- c) A demand to be fed now

Your cat scratches at the door after being fed. Is it saying:

    a) Let me out – I need to use the garden
    b) I want to go out and play
    c) Wonder what they've got to eat next door?

27
REASONS TO OWN A CAT AND NOT A DOG

1. Cats rule. Dogs drool.

2. Cats rub your leg when they want affection, not when they're randy.

3. Cats use a litter box. Dogs use your leg.

4. In 1996, over 10,000 US deaths were attributed to dog owner's choking on saliva during morning wake-up licks.

5. Cats always land on their feet. Dogs won't even let you throw them.

6. Cats let you kick them when you're stressed out.

7. Cats will wait until you've read your morning paper before tearing it to shreds.

8. Cats look cute sleeping on the TV. Dogs crash right in front of the screen.

9. No one has ever had to 'Beware of the Cat'.

10. Cats bury their jobbies. Dogs dig up others'.

11. Cats have better things to do than stick their nose in your crotch.

12. Cats lie on the car in the heat. Dogs in heat lay the car.

13. Why do you think they call it 'Dog Breath?'

14. Garfield. Pluto. Enough said.